CHORTLES

CHORTLES

NEW AND SELECTED WORDPLAY POEMS

EVE MERRIAM

———————— ILLUSTRATIONS BY ————————

SHEILA HAMANAKA

MORROW JUNIOR BOOKS / NEW YORK

The Publisher acknowledges permission to reprint "Portmanteaux" (page 53) from *A Word or Two with You* by Eve Merriam. Copyright © 1981 by Eve Merriam. All rights reserved. Reprinted by permission of Atheneum Publishers, Inc., a division of Macmillan, Inc., and the author.

A number of poems in this book appeared previously in *There Is No Rhyme for Silver*, *It Doesn't Always Have to Rhyme*, *Out Loud*, and *Rainbow Writing*.

All requests for permission
to quote excerpts from the book
should be addressed to Eve Merriam,
c/o Marian Reiner,
71 Disbrow Lane, New Rochelle, N.Y. 10804.
All other requests to reproduce the book
should be addressed to
William Morrow & Company, Inc.,
105 Madison Avenue,
New York, N.Y. 10016.
Printed in the United States of America.
2   3   4   5   6   7   8   9   10
Library of Congress Cataloging-in-Publication Data
Merriam, Eve
Chortles : new and selected wordplay poems/by Eve Merriam ;
drawings by Sheila Hamanaka.
p.   cm.
Summary: A collection of poems focusing on unusual words and plays
on words.
ISBN 0-688-08152-5.   ISBN 0-688-08153-3 (lib. bdg.)
1. Children's poetry, American.   [1. American poetry.]
I. Hamanaka, Sheila, ill.   II. Title.
PS3525.E639C48   1989
811'.54—dc19   88-29129   CIP   AC

For Joyce and Lou
E.M.

CONTENTS

CHORTLES

JOKER

There's a flicker of a snicker
before Joe tells a joke,
there's a twitter of a titter,
a smiley wily poke,

a trickle of a tee-hee,
a huff of a guffaw,
a snippet of a giggle-snort,
a half of a hee-haw,

a chortle, a chuckle,
a gargantuan grin,
a hoo-hoo-hoo *Ha* HA!
and then he'll begin.

MR. ZOO

He's a lionhearted man,
he's a road hog in his car,
he's a bear for work,
he can outfox you by far.

He's sheepish, he's mousy,
he pussyfoots around,
he ferrets out secrets,
he's a sniffing newshound.

Sometimes he looks owlish,
he's dog-tired at night,
he weeps crocodile tears,
has a wolfish appetite.

He turns gooseflesh when he's cold,
he's piggish as can be,
he's a muttonhead, he's harebrained,
he's a mulish, busy bee.

He's bullheaded, cocksure,
eagle-eyed and alas,
he's a cat's-paw, a loan shark,
a snake in the grass.

His wife is a vixen,
she's a nag, she's a shrew,
she's a social butterfly
who acts kittenish with you.

She's doe-eyed, she's slothful,
she crows a lot, too:
no wonder she's married
to a man like Mr. Zoo!

GREEN WITH ENVY

"I,"
stalks the pale asparagus,
"have green fingernails."

"My hair,"
tops the carrot,
"is green."

"Only I,"
lettuce leaves for the last,
"have a heart of green."

AA COUPLE OF DOUBLLES

1

What is a *llano*?
Is it a hill? Ah no,
it's plain as can be
and grassy.

2

If the aardvark
haad aa caar
aand went out aafter daark,
he might find it haard
to paark.

BY THE SHORES OF PAGO PAGO

Mama's cooking pots of couscous,
Papa's in the pawpaw patch,
Bebe feeds the motmot bird,
and I the aye-aye in its cage,

Deedee's drinking cups of cocoa
while he's painting Dada-style,
Gigi's munching on a bonbon
(getting tartar on her teeth),

Toto's drumming on a tom-tom,
Fifi's kicking up a cancan,
Jojo's only feeling so-so
and looking deader than a dodo,

Mimi's dressing in a muumuu,
Nana's bouncing with her yo-yo,
stirring batter for a baba,
Zaza doesn't make a murmur,

Kiki hopes her juju beads
will help to ward off tsetse flies,
Lulu's looking very chichi
in a tutu trimmed with froufrou:

does all this mean our family's cuckoo?

LLUDE SIG KACHOO

Wed flowers bloob
with sweet perfube
or sdowflakes fall
upod the growd
as dature bakes
its yearly rowd:
subber,
autub,
widder,
sprig:
the cobbod code
its gerbs
doth brig.

AELOUROPHILE

Tabby or tom
serene   calm

creamy as silk
quiet as milk

lapper
napper

a purrer
a petter
sweet kitten begetter

playful
unstrayful

self-made rug
a furry hug
welcome mat

AELOUROPHOBE

Tom or tabby
snarling   grabby
hisser   pouncer
flouter   flouncer

a spitter
a spatter
a scritchit   scratchit

tangle a basket

growler
prowler
hownowmeowler

drat
scat

GAZINTA

There's a strange sort of bird of a word
that abides near the Great Divide;
a gazinta is this bird absurd.

And here is how it got its name:
two gazinta four two times,
and four gazinta eight the same.

PARKING LOT FULL

a much of motors
an over of drives
a choke of carburetors
a flood of engines
a plethora of wheels
a googol of gas tanks
a total of exhausts

CACOPHONY

Garbage truck
sings its song:

"Mash, smash,
grink, chong,

goopidy guck,
grabbid slee,

garrup garruck,
pfoo skree
               bluck."

TWOGETHER

A teaming,
a tandem,
a duet,
a tête-à-tête,

a twain of ears,
a pair as in sleeves,
a brace of doves,
a doubling
(see eyebrows,
nostrils and gloves),

bicycle wheels,
hands on clocks,
a coupling of boot heels,
a mating of socks.

UNFINISHED KNEWS ITEM

A well-known knavish knight with knobby knees
had a knack of knotting his knapsack
while he knelt in his knickerbockers.
One day he knocked his knuckles with a knife,
but knobody knoticed what happened knext. . . .

THE HIKER

Backpacking Max,
past racks of shacks,
past all trail tracks,
bushwhacks,
thwacks,
with an ax
hacks.

Mosquito attacks,
bites through his slacks.

Max,
lax,
too late the bug smacks—

cracks open
his rucksack's
stack of Snackpacks.

MISNOMER

If you've ever been one
you know that
you don't sit the baby,
you bouncer
stander
holder
halter
puller
patter
rocker
feeder
burper
changer
kisser
bedder.

A NUMBER OF WORDS

wanton

to-do

threne

forfend

fiveling

sixain

sevenbark

aitchbone

nighness

tenet

AMPHIBIAN

Heavy-footed trot o'mus,
in the river spot o'mus,
golly, what a lot o'mus,
hippo, hippopotamus.

RESOLUTION

My mind is a catchall,
a hodgepodge of ragtag
that's tangled pell-mell,
a snarl, a snag,
a clutter, a jumble,
a rummage, a grab bag,
tatterdemalion,
in disarray.
On the next rainy day
I'll get it cleared away.

ATTIRE

How will you dress for the costume ball?

Clad in crinoline with cincture,
calico kimono,
farthingale of organdy,
redingote of duvetyn?
In a sari of madras, poncho of baize?
A dhoti, dashiki, a kilt with serape,
breeches and buskins,
gaiters and galluses?
Jodhpurs of twill,
a damask doublet,
toga or tutu of tulle?
In epaulets or mufti with ascot and cummerbund
topped with a porkpie over it all?

THE EGOTISTICAL ORCHESTRA

Vaunts violoncello,
"I'm a fine fellow."

Boasts bass,
"I'm the ace."

Flaunts French horn,
"Sans moi, all's forlorn."

Pipes flute,
"I'm some sweet toot."

Brags piano, "I'm both upright *and*
grand."

Snoots cymbal, "My crashing
is simply smashing."

Vies xylophone,
"I set a high tone."

Raps baton, "Come on,
knock off the cacophony,
get Bach to Tchaikovsky,
I'll call the tune."

WINDSHIELD WIPER

fog smog	fog smog
tissue paper	tissue paper
clear the blear	clear the smear
fog more	fog more
splat splat	downpour
rubber scraper	rubber scraper
overshoes	macintosh
bumbershoot	muddle on
slosh through	slosh through
drying up	drying up
sky lighter	sky lighter
nearly clear	nearly clear

clearing clearing veer
clear here clear

THE SAPPY HEASONS

In the skue-bly sprays of ding
when yaffodils are dellow,
and tragnolia mees are mellow;
then I feel a fively lellow,
fively lellow.

In the good old tummer-sime,
when lovers spike to loon,
and molden is the goon;
then I hum a tappy hune,
tappy hune.

When the autumn teaves are lurning
and there's lost upon the frand,
still Thanksgiving's hose at cland;
so I'm feeling grimply sand,
grimply sand.

When the winter blorms are stowing
and the snow is hiling pigh,
and nothing dreems to sy;
then I'm glad that ug am snI,
ug am snI.

SERENDIPITY

If you are knightly on your daily way
to slay a dragon
and by that way
you spy a wagon
filled with jewels to the top-tippety,
that is serendipity.

Or if you are Adam adamantly out to do your duty,
and along your macadam route you encounter a
    beauty
who causes your heart to go flop-flippety,
that event is serendipity.
Sir, meet Lady Serendipity.

Wherever you search for thorns and turn up a
    rose,
there is that fortune you cannot importune:
there is where fair serendipity grows.

A FISHY SQUARE DANCE

Tuna turn,
flounder round,
cuttlefish up,
halibut hold;

clam and salmon
trout about,
terrapin,
shrimp dip in;

forward swordfish,
mackerel back,
dace to the left,
ide to the right;

gallop scallop,
mussel perch,
grunion run,
bass on down;

finnan haddie,
skate and fluke,
eel and sole,
shad and roe;

haddock, herring,
hake, squid, pike:
cod promenade
and lobster roll!

RIGMAROLE

A glimmer,
a glamour,
a magical spell:
the wishing star
fell into the well.
Swim,
swum,
kipple a kipper,
toll the bell
and fetch the Big Dipper.

TEAM WORDS

A mixture a mingle
a sleigh bell a jingle
a valley a dingle
a rooftop a shingle
a hearthside an ingle
a glowing a tingle

POLYGLOT

All over the world
with each day's borning,
the cock crows
Good Morning.

In Russian it goes
kukareku.
In France it cuts through
as *cocorico*.
On the banks of the Po
it's *chicchirichi*.
Wachst Du auf in Germany;
can't you hear the cock crow
kikeriki?
In Vietnam the herald of dawn sounds *cuc-cu*.
In Tokyo,
kokekkoko.

Wake up,
it's daybreak,
may all go well,
cockadoodledoo,
wherever you dwell.

ITINERANT

Please please what is your pleasure?
Whatever will please you I'll make to your measure:
a garment   a vesture   a costume to suit.

Blue jeans with patches cut out of clouds
sandals that skip every stone in the road
pockets that deepen to hold all your dreams
a knapsack of notions to lighten your load.

Please please what is your pleasure?
Whatever will please you I'll make to your measure:
a wardrobe   a dressing   raiment to boot.

A cloak of the night with a lining of stars
a shirt made of music (the buttons sing bass)
a kerchief of lilacs to whiff as you sniff
magic and marvels to match you apace.

Please please what is your pleasure?
Whatever will please you I'll make to your measure:
a cover   a comfort   a habit to suit.

GAB

Yap yawp palaver prattle
natter patter chatter and drone
buzz buzz a snippet of gossip:
I just overheard on the telephone.

Yap yawp palaver prattle
natter patter chatter and prate
tssk tssskk a tittle of tattle:
They say he came home most fearsomely late.

Yap yawp palaver prattle
natter patter chatter and rant
bib bub a babble of boredom:
One of her curtains is hanging aslant.

Yap yawp palaver prattle
natter patter chatter and drone
ooh aaah a peering of prying:
What do they do when they're all alone?

THE ULTIMATE PRODUCT

Chomp,
chew,
munch,
crunch
no-drip no-slip easy-grip
lip-smacking dip and sip
finer designer
potato chip.

I'M SORRY SAYS THE MACHINE

I'm sorry says the machine,
Thank you for waiting says the tape recording,
Trying to connect you says the voice at the
  end of the line.

I'm sorry that sister is not in working order.
Please verify your brother and try him again.
I'm sorry that mother is out of service.
Thank you for waiting, that father you have
  reached is a temporary disconnect.

I'm sorry that landlord is not in working order.
Please verify your neighborhood and try it again.
I'm sorry those repairs are out of service.
Thank you for waiting, that official you have
  reached is not reachable at this time.

I'm sorry that water is not in drinking order.
Please verify that sunlight and try it later.
I'm sorry that blue sky is out of service.
Thank you for waiting, those flowers and trees
  are permanently disconnected.

I'm sorry that country is not in working order.
I'm sorry that planet is out of service.
Please verify that godhead and try much later.
Thank you for waiting, that universe has been
  dis—

A TOKEN OF UNSPOKEN

Some words get read,
but seldom said.

I regret to say
that's true
of *rue*.

While it may be berated,
objurgated
remains unstated.

Furthermore, in debate
I may equivocate,
yet I've never been heard to
tergiversate.

I hope you won't mind
all this *inveighing*:
that, to be sure,
goes without saying.

KUDZU

When kudzu seed the sower sows,
how it grows and overgrows.

Starting in one garden plot,
soon it's in the next-door lot,

twining round the neighbors' door,
creeping to their second floor,

at their chimney, climbing higher
to TV's antenna wire,

past the church's topmost spire,
kudzu to the sky and skyer.

RODOMONTADE IN THE MENAGERIE

I'm the goose
that lays golden eggs.

I'm the cow
that jumps over the moon.

I'm the worm
that swallowed the robin.

I'm the wolf
that cries "Boy!"

I'm the cat
with ten lives.

I'm the
living dinosaur.

DESCENT

come down from the moon
  from mountains
    from towers
      from treetops
        from crags
          from cliffs
            from slopes
              from hillocks

from plateaus   from hummocks
  from cobbles   from mesas
    from rises   from knolls
      from ridges
        from bushes
        from hedges
            to plains
            to valleys
            to trenches
            to ditches
            to marshes
            to swamps
            to fens
            to ponds
            to seaweed
            to plankton
            to coral
            to sponge   exuding breathing
            breathing out bubbles
            round as the moon

EUPHEMISTIC

Ahem
hem-haw
hesitate
commiserate

alasalack   sad to relate
at the age of one hundred and ninety-eight
great-great-great-great-Uncle Clyde
has

breathed his last
passed away
gone to his eternal rest
laid down his burdens
been gathered to his fathers
departed this vale
left us all
shuffled off this mortal coil
answered the trumpet's call
gone O Lord to his heavenly reward
become the late lamented

that is to say,
yesterday

great-great-great-great-Uncle Clyde
finally
died.

WHODUNNIT

Cook in a dudgeon, aggrieved against the boss,
marinating toadstools in the mushroom sauce?
Butler with a bludgeon?
Reaver with a cleaver?
Valet in the alley with a sudden sally?
Chauffeur with a shovel shrouded in a ditch?
Carpenter with flitch crouching in a niche?
Nanny with a needle newly from her knitting?
Granny with a diaper pin for her baby-sitting?
Gardener with a gunnysack by the greenhouse door?
Vicar with an ice pick in the vestry drawer?

Though each behaved suspiciously, both after and
    before,
it was none of the above that brought about the gore.
The villain and the murder weapon used to score?
The host at the party—with a deadly bore.

UN-NEGATIVE

Although affirmative goals I sought,
all my efforts have gone for naught:

attempting to do as I was taught,
I became positively graceful,
my wardrobe well kept;

still no one calls me
corrigible,
kempt,
or ept.

EGO-TRIPPING

1
"I'm,"
declared IM,
"perial,
portant,
perative,
manent.

I'm peding,
I'm pelling,
I'm puting,
I'm plicate.

I'm ploring;
what's more,
I'm mune
and I'm mersed—
by my oath,
I'm precate."

2
"I only,"
said IN,
"sinuate. . . .
Just quiring if you would please dicate:

Are you dustrious,
telligent,
sured?
Dividual,
tuitive,
trigued,
flated,
ured?

Do you dulge, volve or struct,
sult, ject, tegrate?
Terpret, terrupt, troduce, timidate?
Vade, veigh, voke, hibit,
tercede, vestigate?
As a matter of terest, I terrogate:
if you're so clined,
kindly check and fill
IN!"

PARENTHESES

a set of bookends where
the volumes in between
are private

(no one is to read this except you)

DITTO MARKS or,
HOW DO YOU AMUSE A MUSE?

How do you amuse
        " "

when intent
       " " she skulks,
wearing a furbelow
with   " " " ?

If she's sulky often
at quarter   " " ,
roll out the red carpet
and give her a   " " ;
if still she's standoffish,
try platters   " "

POSTCARDS

1

&

we are camping in the romantic land
of Ampersand!
aromatic with camphor
&
sandalwood
&
ample groves of Academe
but damp
nothing dries out
&
there are lampreys

2

the rivers are still
no breeze
the birds have concrete wings
unable to rise
in
this state of
Inertia

3
How shall I describe
PARAPHERNALIA?

Hard to sort out impressions—
the foothills are cluttered—
coast not clear—

statue of the great goddess
hacked into tourist souvenirs:
Paraphernalian ashtrays, pendants, dolls,
bumper stickers, buttons, bikinis, tote bags,
key rings, corkscrews, balloons, banners, beach balls.

4
A quick stopoff at Quaff.
One longs to drink it all in,
but no time to linger,
we must get on to
Gulp.

NOTIONS

Shoelaces
clever as a politician

there are strings that can be pulled
everything can be tied up

Socks
timid
afraid of falling down

give us a hand
help us to stand on our own feet

Belt
class-conscious neutralist
dividing line between
upper and lower

Buttons
unable to bear a single life
always looking for a match

Pants
smug wisdom

no matter if you put your best foot forward
in the end
it's all one and the same

T-shirt
independent
wearing no man's collar

Cap
a closed mind

Wallet
telling the inside story

THE SERPENT'S HISS

        sliding over stones
        a silent spill

    sleek as silk
    iridescent

appearing and
disappearing

     slipping soundless out of sunlight
     to seek dark-wooded sanctuary

        sequestered
        surreptitious

          slithering round
          underground secretive roots

        Narcissus

    spun in upon
    its sinuous self

ancient synonym for
    sibylline
        mystery

BEWITCHERY

Pox,
pox,
a pox
on socks.

Washing machine
takes in two:
only one
comes back to you.

DUSK

daylight is drifting
a dapple
a dawdle

tarry unharried
a slither
a loiter

in dalliance
lingering
reconnoiter

amble a ramble
skimble-scamble
a skimmer   stone-skipper

still fish in the river
still graze in the meadow
still gather the roses

go loping
go lolling
hammocking glide

creeping as lizard
yawning as
          f   e   a   t   h   e   r

a languor
a steeping
twilight's forever

darkness comes later
later much later
(a moment from now)

CROWD

poke prod
poke prod
poke prod
push shove
push shove
shove poke
jostle   push   thrust   shove
nudge   nudge   poke   prod
crush stomp jostle trod
trod trod throng Trod
poke prod poke prod mass push thrust shove
shovE shove troop shove stomp troop trod trOOp
proD poke shove jam
press press press presspoke stompnudge stomp
jostle proD Nudge nudge nudgE JAb
heel heel elbow knees squeeze crush pack poKe
prod jostle hustle haSSle poke stoMp crush thrusT trOD TROD
massjampacksqueeze nudgecrushprodthruST
heave   heave   HEAVE

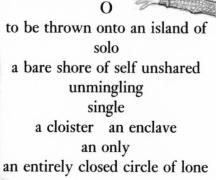

O
to be thrown onto an island of
solo
a bare shore of self unshared
unmingling
single
a cloister   an enclave
an only
an entirely closed circle of lone

PORTMANTEAUX

Two separate words
sometimes condense
into a sound
that's more intense:
pairings like those
are *portmanteaux*.

Thus smoke and fog
roll in as *smog*,
breakfast and lunch
are served for *brunch*,
scatter and hurry blur into *scurry*,
rush and hustle run into *rustle*,
chuckle and snort cavort as *chortle*:
so language like
a giraffe's neck grows.

A turtle that's short
may turn to *tortle*,
a grape and a berry be a *grerry*,
a nest in a nut tree form a *nustle*:

so coin new words
and spend and lend
as syllables wander, waft and wend
and blend and bend and never end.

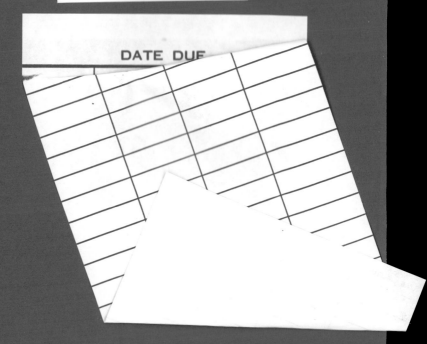

DATE DUE